INTIMACY

UNLEARNING RELIGION – EMBRACING GOD

PETRA F.W. SCOTT

Intimacy

© 2022 Petra F.W. Scott

ISBN 978-1-66785-893-7
eBook ISBN 978-1-66785-894-4

DEDICATION

This book is dedicated to:

The one who knew me before anyone else

The lover of my soul and author of my life

The one who keeps me going and covered in His grace

Who carries me and sets my pace

My source

My strength

My peace and common sense

The one who loved me before I could love myself

Who gave me worth and confidence above everyone else

My best friend

My constant companion

The one who gave it all for me

The one who gives me victory

The one who gives me light when darkness consumes me

To the one who heard my cries when it felt like I was losing

My God, my King, my Everything …

Yeshua, this is for you.

TABLE OF CONTENTS

"A LOVE LETTER TO THE CHURCH"

In this book, I address topics that are very sensitive to believers. I want to let it be known that in no way am I attacking the institution of the church or believers. The entire purpose of this book is to redefine what healthy Christianity looks like through the lens of a relationship. When this happens, the church can be the safehouse, a hospital, and a beacon of hope for the communities we dwell in. If we don't address the issues and take the time to heal the brokenness, then we are ineffective as a spiritual institution.

Salvation is a decision. Spiritual disciplines like prayer, fasting, and worship are rewarding, but intimacy is the believer's choice to go deeper to see into the heart of the Father. Intimacy seals and deepens all the other components of our salvation.

This book is a tool, a revelation of God's heart for his children. The church so beautifully called "the Bride of our Lord" is not meant to be perfect. Still, it is called to be authentic, and genuine authenticity takes place when intimacy is at the core of the identity of the church. We can't be the hands and feet of Jesus if we haven't taken time to establish intimacy. I am pleading with the church; I am using my journey as a means to share what we can become if we prioritize intimacy.

I often ask those I come in contact with, "How are you doing spiritually? How is your relationship with God during this season in your life?" I can't tell you how many times I have gotten one of two responses. The first: "My walk is good. I go to church every week, and I am involved in the ministry." The second: "I haven't been to church in a while, so leave me alone." Both of these answers infuriate me.

Our relationship with God is not measured by church attendance or ministry performance. *It is regulated by intimately engaging in a relationship with God through all seasons and storms.*

We don't have to like the things we may face or the lessons we learn, but intimacy tells us that the Lord is there through it all—nothing is hidden from Him. We cannot compartmentalize our relationship with Him in a box called "church." The very act of doing that is religious. The spiritual institution of the church is there to cultivate the Kingdom community and to enrich the intimacy we individually pursue. The church cannot create a relationship with God; it can only nurture it. The church is the gathering place of those who are crazy in love with the creator of their souls. This book is ultimately my love letter to the body of believers and beyond. It is my cry for us to do better, be better, and function as *one intimate unit.*

-**Petra**

FOREWORD

I love and serve Jesus in what I call the masculine context. I served Promise Keepers for 20 years (10 of them as President) and the U.S. Army for equally as long. I have commanded a company, battalion, and district recruiting command. I served in the Pentagon and Vietnam, pastored two churches, and hold the title of Pastor Emeritus of Rock Church in Chicago.

My point: I consider myself a man's man—a leader who loves the Lord. However, I have always avoided or sidestepped dialogue that referred to an "intimate" relationship with Jesus. Intimacy, to me, was feminine, and my relationship with Jesus was supposed to be masculine.

I have made fun of some Christian songs that reference intimacy in relating to Jesus. I humbly confess now that I was missing a complete, wholesome, precious, and "intimate" relationship with my Lord. What opened my eyes to this reality? Revelation and dialogue with my daughter, which became the substance of this book!

My ability to relate personally to Jesus as he healed the sick, raised the dead, walked on water, and fed thousands was limited. Petra illuminated a human side of Jesus to me that rocked my world and opened the door to a vast missing element in my relationship with Jesus. This revelation introduced me to "intimacy" with my Lord. Oh, if only I had known it when I was pastoring in Chicago!

You cannot teach a closer walk with Jesus until you have a closer walk with Jesus yourself. My intimacy with Jesus is not feminine; it is personal. Powerful and ultimately fulfilling. It makes obedience to the Lord a joy to perform.

I dare you to read this book! You will awaken a new significant, personal, and intimate relationship with the Jewish Messiah. Jesus, the Jewish son who turned water into wine in obedience to his Mother, even though his time had not arrived.

My macho-man, masculine context is not changed; instead, it is now more complete, because it contains personal intimacy. The intimacy reflected when Jesus placed his Mother in care of His friend John while being crucified for the redemption of humanity.

If you are a pastor, spiritual leader, or a warrior for Jesus, this book will give you the roadmap for a closer and more intimate walk with Jesus.

Dr. Raleigh B Washington
President, Awakening the Voice of Truth

INTRODUCTION

As a little girl—a short, bouncy, brown-skinned, long-haired, don't-care pastor's kid from Chicago—one of my favorite things to do was go to church.

There were so many things about it I loved! When it was time to leave for the service, excitement would course through my body. I looked forward to the refreshments after service—the red punch and cheap chocolate and vanilla cookies that always seemed to hit my taste buds just right. And I knew there would be songs to sing and sway back and forth to.

I knew my friends were there waiting to laugh and play with me, and I loved writing secret notes to them on the back of bulletins. I remember how we would mimic and laugh at various things during the service. Plus, I was the pastor's kid, which meant no one could tell me anything (so I thought)! In reality, there was regular chastisement from the serious, no-nonsense ushers.

I also knew all the words to the Benediction and memorized the process of Holy Communion every first Sunday of the month. I knew the words to every song, verses for all seasons, and the process for each tradition and ritual.

All of this was CHURCH, and the related community, family, and friends were an intricate-yet-consistent part of my everyday life.

Yet I still experienced a mysterious distance toward the ONE who we were all there to worship. Now, don't get me wrong; I of course recited the prayer of salvation to Jesus, because you better believe I did not want to go to hell. Despite all of that, Jesus and God the Father seemed distant and unattainable in the world of my church. I couldn't comprehend that a God so big and mighty would care anything about a little Brown girl from the west side of Chicago, Illinois. I was taught that God loved me, and I did fear Him, but I had no independent, intimate connection with Him. I thought that my love for the church and everything about it was my love for God.

Little did I know that this way of thinking was one of the most important life lessons I would need to unlearn.

As I became an adult, I reached a place in my life where mundane religious routines were no longer enough. I was a great member, church leader, speaker, teacher, and sister in the Lord. I attended events and conferences and experienced mountainous highs and valley lows. Throughout it all, I still couldn't shake the feeling that there *had* to be more to the Kingdom of God than what I knew.

Ultimately, I found myself becoming resentful toward Christianity. I felt as though we were reciting scriptures as quotes that sounded cool but had no real power. I felt like we were singing songs because we memorized the words, and the melody was lovely—not because we knew that worship could move mountains. I felt like it was more about social and religious acceptance rather than actual healing and growth.

And so I found myself at a crossroads. I was faced with continuing a mundane religious routine for the rest of my life, which, while helping occasionally, left me empty more than fulfilled. Or, I could begin a journey of pursuing an unknown road … one toward intimacy with God. I chose the latter, and it was terrifying! It was the road less traveled, and it led me to question and challenge every religious ideology upon which I had built my life.

In these pages, you shall learn what I discovered.

You will come with me on a journey of unlearning religion and discovering instead what it means to have an intimate relationship with God. I don't care if you are not a believer, or if you grew up in the church, or if you once associated yourself with Christianity. I invite you all on a journey to redefine your walk of faith.

Before we begin, let us recite this prayer:

"God, I have no idea what lies before me on this journey of unlearning religion. What I do know is that you are with me. Even in times when darkness and doubt try to consume me, you are with me. When I'm going through the motions, when my fears and insecurities try to define me, you are with me. Amid this ocean of religion and the institution of the church, I choose to grab hold of your life raft. I choose to trust you as my lifeguard—the one who guards my life. You and you alone, Lord, are the source that I need … the only consistent source of stability. I choose now to open my soul; I permit you to plow a new road in my soul that will lead me to intimacy with you. It's hard to trust you when I don't know what lies ahead. Despite this, I believe you are all-knowing, all-powerful, a healer, protector, promise keeper, and my Father. Even when I don't feel these things, when my doubt speaks louder than my faith, I will choose to stay the course. I am free to just be your vulnerable child with no strings attached. I release all lies and toxic whispers that try to deter me from the path you have laid before me. I willingly lay down my religious tendencies, offenses, traditions, and ideologies, and today, I choose intimacy above all else.

In Yeshua's name, Amen."

Now, sit back, relax, and inhale God's presence while you exhale your fears. Allow your walls and guards to rest for a moment, and embark with me now …

On a trip toward INTIMACY.

CHAPTER 1:

THE HUMANITY OF JESUS

The first stop on the road to intimacy with Jesus involves understanding the humanity of Jesus. In my religious experience with the church, I discovered that the majority of what I studied, and lessons learned from multiple sermons were all about the work that Jesus had done. I knew the miracles he performed, the disciples he led, his teachings, and, ultimately, his sacrifice on the cross. All of these works and acts were amazing. They shaped Christianity, and they inspire the ministries that Christians do. Still, something was missing ... something was off, for me.

I knew what Jesus *did*, but I didn't know much about *who he was*. I knew him in his divinity well, yet I couldn't tell you much about his humanity.

According to Webster's dictionary, "humanity" is defined as "compassionate, sympathetic, or generous behavior or disposition: the quality or state of being humane; the quality or state of being human." The important thing to grab from this definition is that, because of our God's human form and existence, we have grounds to justifiably connect and relate to Him!

The Biblical context for the Lord's humanity is in Philippians 2:5-8, which states: *"Christ Jesus: who, being in very nature God, did not consider equality with God something to be grasped, but made Himself nothing, taking the very nature of a servant, being made in **human likeness**. And being found in appearance as a man ..."* Understanding this revelation caused me to grab hold of the hand of my Lord, my God. A God who could connect with me in my humanity, because He understood and experienced humanity.

To obtain vulnerability in an intimate relationship, one must have a sense of common ground and connectedness. Understanding the humanity of the Lord is where this begins.

Once I established and ultimately accepted that I needed to dive deeper into the humanity of Jesus, I went straight to scripture for additional insight. Luke 3:23 tells us that Jesus was 30 years old when his cousin John the Baptist baptized him. After the baptism, Jesus fasted for 40 days. Then began his formal ministry for the next three years leading up to his crucifixion.

This revelation blew my mind. I realized that my entire understanding and religious connection to Jesus was all built on the accomplishments he carried out during the last three years of his Earthly life. Upon learning this, I immediately screamed, "No way! You have got to be kidding me." What was he doing for his first 30 years, and why didn't I know anything about it? Why didn't I have any connection to my Lord's first 30 years as a man on Earth? I felt like a child discovering the truth about a parent after a big secret had been withheld from me. As a result of this feeling, I began to dive headfirst into a pursuit of the first 30 years of Jesus's life—the years of his HUMANITY.

Some of you reading this might immediately contest: the Bible only gives us an incredibly small glimpse into the "early years" of Jesus's life.

While this is very true, the little glimpse that it provides offers profound revelations that could very well rock your world, too. Let me give you an example:

Luke 2:41 tells us, *"Every year, his parents went to Jerusalem for the feast of the Passover."* Jesus celebrated Passover *every single year*. It was a formative celebration in his life that helped shape who He was as a man. I couldn't shake the thought that all across the world, Christians proclaim they want to be like Jesus, yet many don't celebrate Passover. How many of us even truly know what Passover really is? Many Christians categorize Passover as a "Jewish only" holiday. They have no connection with it … yet it was a celebration in which our Lord regularly took part! How could it be that we have missed this? How is it that Passover is not part of our regular religious expression in Christianity? This one revelation opens a vast Pandora's box that reveals why the Christian community has missed out on the humanity of our Lord.

There is no way I can understand Jesus, the man, if I don't know that He not only was a Jew, but that everything Jewish was a part of His life.

I realized at that moment that to be intimate with people, you can't just know them for what they do; you have to know them *holistically.*

I didn't know who Jesus was as a JEWISH man (if this is hard for you to accept, keep reading—more on this below). And I didn't know anything about JEWISHNESS.

Let me tell you how good God is. Around the same time that I began my journey on the road to intimacy, my father and his best friend, Coach, started a ministry called the Road to Jerusalem. The entire purpose of the ministry is to help the church realize that they had forsaken their Jewish roots and Messianic Jewish brothers and sisters. The ministry looks to spread the message of ONE NEW HUMANITY: to see Messianic Jews (Jews who accepted Jesus as Messiah) and Gentile (non-Jewish) Christians come together as one—the very thing Jesus prayed for in John 17.

Because of this ministry, I was able to meet and connect with Messianic Jews for the first time in my life. I was able to meet believers who LIVED the humanity of Jesus in present day. I was able to participate in Passover and other biblical feasts that Jesus celebrated. I was able to learn that they called him "Yeshua," the Hebrew name his Mother gave him. And my mind was blown; I was beginning to feel closer to the Lord than I ever had before just by taking a leap of faith and exploring his Jewishness further. There I was on the road, the unknown path to intimacy, which was causing me to unlearn religion in favor of relationship. I was learning about the humanity of my Lord. I was feeling closer to Him. It was no longer about the church routine. I was pulled to dig deeper and discover more about the relationship.

I simply wanted Him for who He was!

I realized that, through the lens of religion, I was contextualizing my Christianity based on what was comfortable to me. I colonized Jesus; I made him a friendly fixture in my African American world. I didn't realize I was doing so until I had this revelation.

Real intimacy doesn't require you to change the culture that shaped you; God didn't make a mistake when he created you in a particular race or ethnicity. The Lord celebrates our differences; they are a part of our humanity. When I had the revelation of the Lord's humanity, the Holy Spirit gave me what I call the "Marriage Analogy":

Marriage Analogy

What if God called you to marry a person who is ethnically and culturally different from you? What if one day, this person said, "Honey, I love you so much. You mean the world to me. I can't wait to spend my life with you, but I have one request. Can you leave your race, ethnicity, and cultural expression out of our marriage? Honey, I just want it to be about our love— not your race and not your people. Just us and our love."

IF I were ever in that predicament, I would say to my potential spouse, "Hit the road, Jack." Who I am as an African American woman directly influences how I see the world ... how I cook, dance, and celebrate life. If you can't embrace, honor, and understand my culture, then how can you completely embrace and love me?

After He revealed this analogy, I shouted, "I GET IT!" In the church, we say we are "the Bride of Christ." Yet we have spoken to the Lord, saying, "We love your miracles and your teachings. We love what you did for us on the cross. But the Jewish feasts that you celebrated every year? Well, we don't need to have anything to do with that. Your Jewish people and the other customs and traditions that helped shape you in the first 30 years of your life? Well, we don't need to understand that, either." As the Bride, we are saying we accept your DIVINITY, but your HUMANITY is not that important. Then, we wonder why so many of us only have a surface relationship with the Lord.

If we don't know him in the FULLNESS of who he is, how can we have an intimate relationship with him?

Now, some of you may still be struggling with the reality of Jesus being Jewish. Let's address it. Why was Jesus chosen to be Jewish? The answer is simple: because our God is a promise-keeper. In the Old Testament, God searched the Earth for someone who wanted to be in a relationship. He was looking for someone to acknowledge him, and Abraham was the only one who wanted to have anything to do with our God. As a result of that relationship, God made a promise—the first covenant—with Abraham. Remember, Jesus is called "the second covenant." Jesus came to redeem what was broken in the first covenant. He came so that the promise would be fulfilled. The Lord used Israel, the smallest nation, to reveal Himself to the world. God is so amazing that the second covenant is extended to Gentiles (non-Jewish), who are grafted in when embracing his son (Romans 11). We are treated as equal Heirs to the promises of God through Abraham.

Eradicating Jesus's Jewishness prevents us from seeing the faithfulness of God and the intentionality He has toward us.

Am I saying you need to go out and convert to Messianic Judaism to be intimate with our Lord? No. I'm saying that a White man married to a Black woman doesn't become a Black man. Rather, he learns to love, accept, and participate in his wife's culture. Doing so creates greater intimacy in their relationship.

We don't have to become; we have to embrace.

Once this revelation had taken root, I began to sojourn into church history to try and understand how the message could be absent from so many Christian churches and ministries. What I found was alarming and heartbreaking. Then again, it was no surprise. If believers were walking in an intimate relationship with the Lord rather than going through the motions of religious obligation, the church would be more productive. The darkness in this world would begin to fade.

I believe the enemy launched a strategic attack on Christianity when various anti-Semitic early church fathers and leaders significantly impacted how Jesus and his Jewishness is viewed and explained in the church. There is so much to unfold about church history, but below, I briefly explain the key issues that directly affected the church's ability to understand the humanity of our Lord. These concepts/theologies are still present today and hinder unity amongst believers seeking complete intimacy. While there may have been some good that came from some of the references below, the damaging parts cannot be ignored. My aim is not to attack church history, but rather illuminate where man's agenda tries to supersede Gods design for ALL His children.

In knowing them, my hope is that you don't fall prey to them.

The Council of Nicaea: Formed in 325 AD to bring Bishops together to erect standards for the Christian faith. During their gathering, there were several things changed intentionally. Many of the changes revolved around removing certain aspects of our Jewish roots from Christian expression. The council's inability to see the need to keep the Jewish DNA of our faith intact created a breeding ground for the next critical issue.

Replacement Theology/Supersessionism: The church believes that they have replaced Israel as God's chosen people. They believe that the new covenant in the New Testament supersedes the old covenant, which God made with the Jewish people. This theology is like spiritual genocide. If we replaced Israel as "The Church," that would mean our God does not keep his promises. And that goes against the fundamental understanding of our Lord and the seriousness of the covenants He establishes. Replacement Theology is a cancer in Christianity, and we must put an end to it.

Anti-Semitism: Hostility to or prejudice against Jews. Anti-Semitism is pure hatred and often forms when someone has been offended or mistreated by someone of Jewish descent.

Martin Luther's Book: Martin Luther is considered the Father of the Protestant Reformation, which is the launching pad from which many denominations have built their theologies. The issue is that this Father of Protestant Christianity became highly anti-Semitic, even writing a book entitled *On the Jews and Their Lies*, which influenced Hitler's mindset around the Holocaust. In many churches, Martin Luther is praised, which is damaging. Overlooking his vile attack on Jews through his writings and work is damaging to the church's ability to build relationships with our believing Jewish brothers and sisters, and our relationship with them is necessary on the journey toward intimacy with our Jewish Messiah.

Each subject described above has influenced the church and its theology. That is why the concept of really understanding and embracing the humanity of Jesus has been a taboo topic in many Christian circles.

Sometimes, people will acknowledge the Lord's Jewishness, but still fail to make a connection and include it as a part of their faith expression.

To heal, we must admit where we have cracks in the foundation. An inadequate understanding of the Lord's humanity is a crack that can prevent real intimacy. Illuminating the truth builds a new foundation.

In addition to learning more about His Jewishness as a means of further understanding His humanity, scripture also gives us a profound glimpse into the interpersonal aspects of Jesus's humanity. Let's look at Mark 6: 1-6:

> "Jesus left there and went to his hometown, accompanied by his disciples. **2** When the Sabbath came, he began to teach in the synagogue, and many who heard him were amazed. 'Where did this man get these things?' they asked. 'What's this wisdom that has been given him? What are these remarkable miracles he is performing? **3** Isn't this the carpenter? Isn't this Mary's son and the brother of James, Joseph,[a] Judas, and Simon? Aren't his sisters here with us?' And they took offense at him. **4** Jesus said to them, 'A prophet is not without honor except in his own town, among his relatives and in his own home.' **5** He could not do any miracles there, except lay his hands on a few sick people and heal them. **6** He was amazed at their lack of faith."

This passage provides us a glimpse into the reality that Jesus had younger siblings as well as "issues" with friends and relatives in His hometown. He experienced issues coming up that we can relate to in more ways than we may explore on a Sunday morning.

There is this paradigm within Christianity that revolves around only a few being in positions of leadership and teaching, while the majority are in places of sitting and listening. Practices like this lend itself to a very inactive faith experience for the majority of believers. I believe this paradigm exists because many people feel that they are not "holy" enough. That they are inadequate. Many believers have bought into the lie that only those in leadership can have a deep connection with God. Understanding Jesus's humanity in an interpersonal context allows the believer to see that He had real-life drama, struggles, and frustrations. Again, we serve a God who can connect with us in our humanity; He is longing to make that connection with *all* of us, not just those in leadership.

When you have an intimate relationship with the Lord, there is a fresh experience every time you encounter Him. There is a rewarding exchange when you commune with the Father.

The revelation of His humanity opened up a new world for me. Incorporating the Jewish roots of my faith—celebrating the same feasts that my Lord celebrated, doing the same Davidic dances He did, and saying the same prayers and blessings He recited—launched me into a beautiful, grounded, and connected relationship with Him.

As we close this chapter, take some time to reflect on how understanding the humanity of the Lord can re-shape and enhance your faith experience. If you're called to take your learning deeper, refer to the epilogue in the back of the book for resources that can further your knowledge on the humanity of our Lord.

CHAPTER 2:

UNMASKING RELIGION

In this chapter, I want to take a more in-depth look into the Lord's human relationship with God the Father. Still looking at those first 30 years of His life before He began anything formal in ministry, Luke 2:21 says, *"When all the people were being baptized, Jesus was baptized, too. And as he was praying, heaven was opened, and the Holy Spirit descended on him in bodily form like a dove. And a voice came from heaven saying: "You are my son, whom I love; with you, I am well pleased."*

When God the Father said the words, *"You are my son, whom I love; with you, I am well pleased,"* Jesus had not done anything in His formal ministry yet. His only accomplishment thus far was being a faithful SON. It wasn't about what He did; it wasn't about all the miracles, all the teachings, or even the heavy burden of the cross that He would later perform. It was about the INTIMATE RELATIONSHIP, which is what God desires. That is why the Father said to His son—"WITH YOU I AM WELL PLEASED"— *before* He did anything. What a beautiful picture of an intimate relationship laced with unconditional love. In this example any religious notions that we must prove ourselves to earn Gods love are immediately unmasked. We love him because he first loved us.

You can capture the essence of Jesus's relationship with the Father even in His early life. When Jesus and His parents were in Jerusalem, and it was time to leave, they thought He was with them. Except He wasn't, and they were not happy. They looked for Him for three days. When they found Him, he was in the temple learning and teaching, and when they saw Him, we learn through Luke 2:49 that He says, *"Why were you searching for me? Didn't you know I had to be in my Father's house?"* He "HAD" to be in the presence of his Father; it trumped everything. This scripture, my brothers and sisters, is a real picture of intimacy; this was God's son, with whom He was so pleased. Jesus's dedication and faithfulness to be in His presence are evident even when He was a young boy.

Intimacy, real intimacy, is what Jesus shared with God the Father. It was an intimacy that would become the foundation of His ministry.

Within Christianity, there are so many approaches to further one's faith—so many devotions, books, and systems on how to please God and live a better life. My answer to everything is INTIMACY; it's what I believe the Lord desires from us.

Suppose you are still struggling to believe that. Perhaps you feel strongly that He desires our work or intellect through religion. I want you to take your time reading the following:

Mathew 7:21-23 says, *"Not everyone who says to me, 'Lord, Lord,' will enter the Kingdom of heaven, but only the one who does the will of my Father who is in heaven. Many will say to me on that day, 'Lord, Lord, did we not prophesy in your name, and in your name, drive out demons and, in your name, perform many miracles?' Then, I will tell them plainly,* 'I never **knew** you. Away from me, you evildoers!'"

I read this verse, and I was amazed that people who were doing "the work of God" were reprimanded and turned away by God. This concept went against everything I believed or understood. I felt the more you accomplished for the Lord—the outstanding miracles, evangelism, and good deeds—the more likely you were to obtain favor with the Lord.

Yet this passage in scripture illuminates that *your works of righteousness DON'T result in more rubies in your crown or magical favor.* It reveals that it's not about how popular or extensive your ministry is; it's about "knowing him." Once again, I shouted, "Wait a minute. What did these people do wrong?" I was stuck there. I continued studying, and the line in verse 23 would not leave me alone. It haunted me like a scary movie. Before intimacy, my life narrative as a believer consisted of avoiding hell at all costs as the sure way to righteousness! What was it, with this *"I never knew you?"* How could it be that the Lord listed a series of religious events and acts that typically would be seen as great accomplishments, yet cast them aside because *those who were doing these works never "knew" him?* I couldn't help but feel like there was more to this term knew than what I realized, so I studied it. Here is what I found:

In the Strong's Concordance for this particular verse, the reference number for "knew" is **1097** *ginōskō* – properly, *to know*, especially through *personal experience (first-hand* acquaintance). 1097 */ginōskō* ("experientially know") is used for example in Lk 1:34, *"And Mary* [a virgin] *said to the angel,* 'How will this be since I do not *know* (1097 */ginōskō* = sexual intimacy) *a man?'"* (STRONGS)

"Knew" was directly correlated with intimacy ... and not just any intimacy, but the highest form of it. The revelation was evident:

The Lord is not looking for people who perform religious acts and services for others. What He desires most is for us as His children to know Him—to be intimate with Him just as He was with the Father. The goal isn't religious status and pompous achievements. It is intimacy with our Father, and real ministry is what flows from you when the intimacy occurs.

The reason church hurt is so prevalent is that more leaders are leading from a place of religion versus intimacy. When you know the Lord intimately, it's easier to love as He loves, to see as He sees, and to respond as He responds. When you lead from a place of intimacy, you are free from the pressure to be "perfect." You are free from the pressure to produce results as a sign of your success. The Lord is not looking for more religious soldiers trying to further the Kingdom. He is searching to and fro seeking hearts that are genuinely His (2 Chronicles 16:9). This is another picture and scripture denoting that God desires INTIMACY!

The meaning of the word "knew" in this use has the context of sexual/physical intimacy as a part of its definitive property. Sex can be a "taboo" topic in the church, primarily only discussed as one of the top sins to avoid. We teach what's wrong with it, and why it should be avoided by those who are single, young, and dating at all costs. Yet with this topic, there is more fear than understanding.

The church's fear and inability to openly discuss God's turths behind physical intimacy for husbands and wives in all its contexts can aid to the lack of intimate relationships with God. Additionally, it has caused believers to allow the world to govern what physical intimacy is and isn't.

Physical intimacy was created by God as a gift to provide a glimpse of the process and understanding of some of the principles of intimacy. Physical intimacy is sacred, and beautiful. It produces LIFE.

Let me break it down. God does not force Himself upon us; He is a gentleman. We can choose to accept Him as our Lord, but that acceptance is not enough. We have to allow him to break past our walls of fear, hurt, abandonment, rejections, and shame. When we truly allow him to break past those walls, intimacy begins, and intimacy produces life. God can release into us His purpose and plans. When we allow this, we then birth the purpose God has for us.

God needs us to stand boldly—unashamed of who we are and who He has created us to be.

Intimacy should be at the forefront of our faith, rather than a quiet, taboo topic that makes us blush.

Some experiences and circumstances can cause us to be extremely sensitive when it comes to the topic of physical intimacy and our faith. When you have been broken in any sexual way, the last thing you want to do is equate the God you love with something that has caused you so much pain. I believe it is a strategic attack from the enemy to get those of us who have been violated to feel the most threatened within the context of intimacy. What I want to tell you is …

When you allow the Lord to heal even the deepest and darkest of wounds, intimacy with Him becomes a redeeming experience.

You see, what we do with humanity can be great one day and then hated the next. But what we do for the Lord has eternal value. The purpose of this chapter is to highlight the ideology behind this book, which is that the life and personhood of Jesus is our guide for intimacy. This chapter is titled "Unmasking Religion" because when we remove and confront the assumptions we have projected unto God we begin the process of Embracing who He TRULY is.

God is not looking for what you can do or what you have done; He's just looking for you. *You* are the critical ingredient in your intimate connection with the Lord.

CHAPTER 3:

"I DON'T DESERVE INTIMACY"

This chapter speaks to anyone struggling to feel *worthy* of intimacy with the Lord. If you are struggling with the idea that just being a son or daughter is enough, let me give you a picture of why the Lord is not concerned about what you've done, but rather *who you are*.

Let's look at David. One of my favorite passages from David's psalms is Psalm 27:4, which reads:

"One thing I have asked from the Lord, that I shall seek: that I may dwell in the house of the Lord all the days of my life, to behold the beauty of the Lord and to meditate in His temple."

What a breathtaking picture of intimacy between David and the Lord. Notice how he describes how he longs to behold the "beauty of the Lord." David sounds like someone deeply in love and overtaken by intimacy. When I read this passage, and others like it from the Psalms, it became undeniably clear to me why the Lord refers to David as a man after his own HEART. Scripture tells us this twice, in both 1 Samuel 13:14 and Acts 13:22—how exciting that this declaration of God's feelings toward David is in both the Old and New Testament!

The duplicity of this profound statement is to be noted in the life of the believer. David, who is often harshly judged even in the present day for the types of sin he committed, was nevertheless known intimately by the Lord; the Lord knew his heart, and David repented of his ways and served the Lord. David even Loved the Lord so much that he worshipped Him in 2 Samuel 6:14-23 with what is called an "undignified praise," as he was half-naked. People did not like it; they did not think that it was behavior acceptable for a king. It's David's response that blows me away in verse 21:

"It was before the Lord, who chose me rather than your Father or anyone from His house when He appointed me ruler over the Lord's people Israel— I will celebrate before the Lord. 22 I will become even more undignified than this, and I will be humiliated in my own eyes."

Again, the God who created the universe desires to be in an intimate relationship with you! Religion, along with its obligations and comprehensive platform, have gotten in the way of seeing this simple-yet-profound truth. HE LOVES YOU, and HE WANTS YOU, not what you can do. Please don't twist what I am saying; it is good to do things for the Lord. He will lead you to serve and help others in His name. Still, it is not with a yoke of religion or unobtainable expectation. The Lord says in *Matthew 11:28*:

"Come to me, all you who are weary and burdened, and I will give you rest. Take my yoke upon you and learn from me, for I am gentle and humble in heart, and you will find rest for your souls. For my yoke is easy, my burden is light."

Yet so many religious leaders, clergymen, and believers walk around with the most considerable amounts of stress. Intimacy with the Lord doesn't produce stress. It produces REST. *"Who the Son sets free is free indeed"* (John 8:36)—free from the bondage of people-pleasing and pressure from this world, and free to rest in an intimate relationship with the Lord. There are no religions or societal groups that say you don't have to do anything but receive. It's only an intimate relationship with the Lord that produces this level of acceptance, rest, and freedom.

In my own journey, I didn't *earn* the right to be intimate with the Lord. I simply choose to try it. Once I did, I couldn't turn back even if I wanted to, because it's an intimacy that has shaped and fulfilled my life. I dare *you* to try it. Get before the Lord (and no, you don't have to kneel in the traditional sense or take a weird posture—do what is relationally comfortable to you) and say this:

"Lord, I want to see, sense, and hear from you."

He will show up! And you have the choice to engage with Him intimately or not. The Lord is a gentleman; He does not force himself upon us. Even when the disciples didn't understand who He was as Messiah, He was still loving and patient with them.

I love what the Lord tells the disciples in Matthew 8:26. During the storm, when they are in the boat with the Lord after they have already seen Him perform miracles, they scream, "Lord save us," and the Lord responds, "You of little faith, why are you so afraid?" Just like the disciples, some of us have believed in the Lord and looked to His word, but we are afraid to trust Him and engage in intimacy with Him fully. (In the next chapter, I will address more of the roadblocks on our road to intimacy that can cause fear and hinder our journey.)

I, too, once questioned my worthiness of an intimate relationship with God.

When I was 16 years old, I decided to give the Lord a try. I knew I didn't want my faith walk to look like many religious examples of

Christianity I witnessed; I wanted to be different. I wanted to have something real. At 16, I decided to give my life to the Lord to try and see whether all the "Jesus stuff" was real. As a pastor's kid, I didn't like what I saw.

In churches, people often give pastor's kids grief because they expect them to be the standard … what a kid "should" be. That is an unfair expectation to place on a child, so what often happens? They do what most people do when they are put under pressure—fight back and rebel. Pressure plus expectation is a formula for rebellion, and many people don't realize how it applies to the children of those in ministry. We weren't given a choice in the matter, and we surely weren't given the freedom to grow and learn. We were just expected to succeed and perform. I spent much of my adolescence despising my Christian upbringing and falsely judging a God whom I thought wanted to remove anything fun from life. I was also hurt by the things I experienced with those in the church, like the way people treated my parents and siblings. I also experienced abuse that accumulated in an incredible lack of trust in the Christian community. Consequently, I dabbled in other religions, only to find the same pressures of performance and expectation.

That is, until the day, at 16, when I felt the Lord speaking to me. He was reaching out to me on the road to intimacy, and I needed to make a decision. Still, His voice was being drowned out by the loud religious voices I had experienced telling me that I was not worthy or deserving. For reasons I cannot explain, I choose to pursue Him, and this was my first step toward intimacy … toward trying to be a daughter.

We can feel unworthy. We can feel disqualified. But our feelings cannot supersede the truth …

He wants us flaws and all.

Growing up, I would often hear various people say, "God helps those who help themselves." That is a common saying, but it is NOT true, and it is NOT Biblical. If we could help ourselves, then why would we need God?

I believe the intent was to get people to take responsibility for their actions. Still, the truth is, statements and mindsets like that can cause people to feel like they have to get it together *before* they can come to God. Yet He is the one, the *only* one, who can get us together! Sometimes people don't know how to take responsibility for their actions until they have an intimate relationship with God, wherein the Lord can expose and reveal where we were wrong. He can show us how to live right.

If you deeply struggle with believing that you do not deserve intimacy, pray this prayer with me:

> *"God, I recognize that I am afraid of intimacy with you. I am fearful of failing and not living up to the expectations that you or others may have of me. Right now, I am choosing to release the lie that I don't deserve intimacy. I choose to embrace the truth that you want me and all of my baggage and mess. I welcome the fact that just being your son or daughter is ENOUGH! I lay down all negative things that others have spoken over me, or I have spoken over myself. I am yours, and I am perfected in you.*
>
> *In Yeshua's name, Amen."*

CHAPTER 4:

"ROADBLOCKS"

Some of you reading this book may feel that you have tried to move past religion and pursue intimacy, but it's not working; you don't feel that connection. Well, I can relate. It's part of the journey.

In this chapter, I want to address roadblocks on the road to intimacy. Everything is not always black and white, and there are many instances when individuals have a unique circumstance that comes along and blocks intimacy with the Lord. Let's take a look at a few.

Church Hurt:

Often, people experience deep hurt and pain from those in the church. People have been abused (sexually, physically, and emotionally), slandered, shunned, and abandoned by those representing the church. That is not acceptable, and it needs to cease. The real danger occurs when those who have been hurt by the church/Christians begin to project onto God the treatment they received from those who call themselves "His people."

To effectively have intimacy with the Lord, we have to separate the Lord from the people.

I understand this firsthand. As a pastor's kid, I have seen the good, the bad, and the ugly of the church. I have experienced abuse, slander, and abandonment from those in the church. It all caused me to resent it and become bitter toward God.

I did not write this book to present a fairytale picture of what it means to pursue and experience intimacy with God. I wrote it because I know what it's like to live in pain from the things that others do to you, and I know what it's like to live apart from God because you hold Him responsible for it. I projected the actions of religious people on a relational God.

But when I experienced God outside of the pain caused by religious people, I was able to undergo real and profound healing that cultivated an intimacy I can share with others. My best advice here? Forgive the church and any Christians who have wounded you. Those who hurt you are in deep need of intimacy with the Lord.

Parental Pain:

Fathers and mothers are our first understanding of covering and protection. What they do and how they treat their children directly affects how their children will perceive God the Father. If someone experiences abandonment/rejection, abuse, or shame from a parent early in life, it affects their ability to trust others and the Lord completely.

When I was in college, I led a discipleship group called Women of Intimacy. It was birthed out of my desire to see young women, my peers, intimately in love with the Lord. I started the group with my best friend and two of our roommates. When we began, our small college apartment was filled with a little over 20 ladies. I was nervous before the first meeting, so I fasted and went to the park by our campus to seek the Lord. When I got there, I asked the Lord, "What do you have for your daughters?" Immediately, I had a vision. It was of a glass with crystal-clear water; but then, all of a sudden, chunks of dirt, sand, and other materials started to fill the glass. It completely polluted the water. The Lord then spoke to me:

"My daughters have a hard time connecting with me intimately, because their perception of me is polluted. Daughter, I need you to help them filter the water, so they can see me."

I then asked the Lord how in the world might I do that? He said:

"Start with your fathers; your fathers are your first picture of God, whether they are in your lives or not. How you see your earthly Father(s) directly affects how my daughters see me. You can't be a woman of intimacy if you can't know the lover of your soul."

What then unfolded was a practical way for us to filter. That is what the Lord gave me.

I went back to my group and gave each person a piece of paper for every Earthly father they had (in some cases, people have stepfathers or uncles/grandfathers who are surrogate fathers when a biological father is not in the picture). However, even if someone's biological father was not in his or her life, there was still a piece of paper for him. Additionally, there was a piece of paper for the Lord. The instructions were as follows:

For each father, including the Lord, write the following words at the top of the paper:

This is how I view my father: _____. On that paper, the women were instructed to be completely transparent about how they saw and experienced each particular father. After the Earthly fathers were completed, they repeated the process for the Lord.

Before we started, I prayed that each of us would be completely honest and transparent on our papers, no matter how difficult it was. Once this exercise was completed, I then prayed another prayer asking the Father to come and give us a filter. Once that prayer was complete, we finished the second-to-last step, which was to compare how we viewed our fathers with how we saw the Lord. *This* was when revelation occurred. (Note: this exercise is not gender-specific. It has been impactful in the lives of men and women alike.)

During the exercise, there were so many different reactions and feelings from the participants. Despite their unique experiences with their Earthly father(s), what I discovered is that there are generally five types of fathers and five types of intimacy complexes we can develop from them. Below is a breakdown of each.

Present Father: This is the father in the home, but he might be controlling or harsh. Often, the children feel like they have their father's presence, but not his affection or attention. They often feel like they are not good enough for that father, and that nothing they do seems right. That can develop a strained relationship, and as a result of having this type of father, an intimacy complex can occur.

Intimacy Complex: An individual with a present father can know the Lord, but feel as if he or she will never obtain righteousness or holiness. These individuals feel as if they can never measure up spiritually. And often, they feel that if anything goes wrong in their life, it's because they weren't good enough for God, or because they failed spiritually. Those with a present father can struggle to receive the Lord's affections and attention. They wrestle with the realization that they don't have to do anything to please the Lord—that He loves them just for who they are.

Cool Father: This is the father who takes a friendly approach with his child, provides material needs, and shows affection and attention to his child. This father is lax with discipline and firm structure, but he loves and gives when he can.

Intimacy Complex: One might say this father sounds perfect; why would someone have an intimacy complex if s/he had this type of father? Well, this is actually one of the most dangerous forms of an intimacy complex. Individuals with a "cool" father may not feel the need to go deep in their relationship with God. They might feel like they get all they need from their Earthly father, so there is no need to get it from our heavenly Father. These individuals tend to idolize their Earthly fathers, which pushes the heavenly Father away. If something happens and the cool father does something wrong, or if he dies or doesn't perform or provide, then the child can become consumed with anger or bitterness with the Earthly father and with the Lord.

Two ladies in my group had this intimacy complex, and they both were shocked to realize how shallow their relationship with God was because they were so dependent on their Earthly father. They also separately admitted that if something were to ever happen to their Earthly father, they would fall apart and most likely be furious with God the Father. This revelation helped them to put God on the throne and to recognize that we should never idolize the man. We need to be able to lean on something that can never fail—something constant—and that only comes from the Lord.

Absent Father: The absent father is either an unknown father or a known-yet-removed Father. The absent father does not provide financially or emotionally. Individuals with absent fathers often struggle with rejection, abandonment, and feelings like "What's wrong with me? Why couldn't my father choose to be a part of my life? What did I do wrong?" These individuals can become consumed with bitterness and hatred toward the absent father. They become independent and guarded. It's hard for them to believe people's words; they tend to need to see action to validate love.

Intimacy Complex: Individuals with an absent father can have one of two kinds of intimacy complexes. The first is that they may feel as if God is a joke—this "being" who makes a bunch of empty promises while forsaking His children. These individuals can often lean toward feelings reflected in questions like, "If God is real, and if He is good, why do bad things happen to good people?" They tend to see the pain and negativity in the world, and they feel it exists because of God's absence. They often carry bitterness and hatred toward God. The other intimacy complex is that the individual may not be bitter with God. Instead, he or she tends to like God's teachings and may even be regular churchgoers. Still, they do not entirely trust the Lord. They are in favor of charity and kindness, but trusting the Lord wholistically is a little bit "overly spiritual" for them. God has His place, but they don't feel that intimacy is something tangible for them. They tend to be self-reliant and self-sufficient, keeping authority figures at bay. Individuals with absent fathers have a hard time receiving God's adoption and inheritance over their lives. They believe in God, but feel we have to fend for ourselves. The Lord longs to hold His children who have absent fathers. He longs to fill the void of the "orphan spirit." He wants to validate them, so they can be aware of His constant, unfailing presence in their lives. He recognizes that it's hard to feel His presence when what you know from a father is absence. When those who have absent fathers make the decision to engage with the Lord's presence and trust Him relentlessly, they often become some of the most influential in the Kingdom of God.

Abusive Father: When individuals have experienced sexual, physical, spiritual, or mental/emotional abuse at the hands of their Earthly father, they tend to be fragile, and that fragile state can manifest in one of two ways: they can be sensitive, timid, quiet, and isolated, or impulsive and reckless, leaning toward wild behaviors or addictions. The abusive father dehumanizes their child, making him or her feel unworthy of love, respect, and understanding. These actions will shut the child down or drive the child crazy. When the abuse dehumanizes you, you perpetually feel as if you are not enough. You become consumed with shame—and shame is a prison that directly separates the individual from experiencing intimacy with the Lord.

Intimacy Complex: This individual can have one of two kinds of intimacy complexes: first, they can utterly despise God and blame Him directly for their pain and abuse. They tend to find temporary comfort from darkness, be it dark music, movies, images, or patterns of thinking. The other side of the complex for this individual is that they ONLY trust God. They feel that He is the only one who is safe. While safety with God is real, intimacy with God can be blocked if unforgiveness is still in the heart of the child of an abusive father. For some, the idea of forgiving an abusive father is unfathomable. BUT, if forgiveness doesn't take place, it will consume the individual. Unforgiveness can manifest in our bodies in the form of anxiety, which can lead to severe depression, stress, nerve pain, and muscle issues, as well as various other sicknesses.

Christian neurologist Dr. Caroline Leaf wrote a book entitled *Toxic Thoughts*. In it, she explains how negative thinking and feelings directly affect our bodies. The Lord desires to pour out His unconditional redeeming love on His children who have experienced abuse. The question of the child afflicted with abuse is, "Why me?"

The answer to that question is found in the cross. The Lord gives all humanity free will—meaning, we have the freedom to choose Him or not. God doesn't force us to do anything. He is sovereign, but He is not a dictator. He searches for those who love Him. As I explained in Chapter 2, He doesn't force us to serve and love him, and just like we have a choice to serve Him, others have the option to do wrong. Sometimes, we are on the receiving end of their evil actions. Still, God said, *"That's why I sent my son to redeem the evil that was done to you. I sent Him to take the ashes and give you beauty (Isaiah 61:3). To take all things and work them together for your good (Romans 8:28). To promise you eternal life when you trust me, so that your present suffering will not compare to the glory that will be revealed when you are with the heavenly Father in eternity (Romans 8:18)."* I believe that God can produce purpose from our pain. I believe that He is sovereign. Still, I also believe that suffering is part of our humanity. God sent Jesus, and He suffered, and He struggled, but He knew that there were purpose and fulfillment on the other side of the pain.

Don't let the pain of abuse consume you; trust me, I understand, and there is HOPE. I have seen what God does when the abused child breaks free from shame and walks into bold, royal confidence in who he or she is in God; s/he becomes an unstoppable force that changes the world!

Distant Father: The distant father is the father who may be there every other weekend or less. The one you hear from on birthdays or holidays. The one who may make an occasional sporting event, but has no real responsibility other than child support. The distant father is one you have hope of knowing better, but never feel like it's attainable.

Intimacy Complex: Often, individuals with distant fathers tend to approach their relationship with God in the same way their fathers approached parenting: "I'm cool with God. I go to church occasionally. I pray periodically. Read a Christian book here and there. I listen to a YouTube message every once and a while." But there is no real commitment ... no solid, sold-out love affair with the Lord. Rather, there's just enough to feel like they're getting by. Sometimes, those with distant fathers can fall into religious patterns that are centered on being overly committed. Because they have not experienced devout commitment, even this does not fill their void of intimacy. Sometimes, the children of distant fathers can place massive expectations on God and others. When those expectations aren't met, they tend to pull away from the Lord and others in the Lord. That creates a wall.

The Lord wants the individuals with distant fathers to grasp the truth that He will never leave nor forsake them (Hebrews 13:5). He wants these children to know the fact that they don't have to worry or be anxious about anything (Philippians 4). He wants them to see that He realizes that a distant father brings uncertainty and inconsistency, which can cause children of distant fathers to feel like they need to be in control ... and trying to be in control only produces anxiety and other issues. He sees. He cares. And HE is in control.

No matter which category or intimacy complex the participants of my group fell into, there was a need to filter, so they could see the Lord. Additionally, as I mentioned earlier, this was not a gender-specific exercise, and it's been amazing to see how these categories and intimacy complexes do not change based on gender. The soul is impacted the same way.

While that exercise was geared toward fathers, the next is around our experiences with our mothers. In the group, we explored how they have influenced our interaction and perception of the Holy Spirit. I initially put together the father categories out of an overwhelming realization of how deeply we all needed to filter through our father issues to have fulfilling intimacy with the Lord. But I've also encountered various clients and mentees who had just as many problems with their mothers, which is why the Holy Spirit had me do a similar exercise.

The Holy Spirit is our comforter and guide—an identical role to that of a mother. Below are the categories of mothers, and instead of an intimacy complex, you will find a corresponding Holy Spirit complex. An intimacy complex is directly related to our view and interactions with God. A Holy Spirit complex is directly related to God at work within us, and how we treat and relate to others.

People-Pleasing Mother: This mother does it all by herself; she goes above and beyond to be the best mother she can be, but she neglects herself in the process. She blames herself for every shortcoming her children have. She will sacrifice anything, including her health, to see her children happy. This mother has no boundaries for self-care.

Holy Spirit Complex: An individual who has a people-pleasing mother can develop issues with embracing God's rest and grace. They often live a stressful and busy life. The Holy Spirit wants them to break free from fear of man and pleasing man. Proverbs 29:25 says, *"The fear of man lays a snare, but whoever trusts in the Lord is safe."* Don't be afraid to follow your dreams; don't sacrifice your purpose. Living your purpose does better for those in your life.

Superwoman Mother: This headstrong mother works, takes care of her children, and may have a high level of education or regularly takes classes. She likely enjoys an active social life and extra-curricular activities. She shops, cooks, and cleans for the family, and she is fit and focused. She plans activities, schedules appointments, and handles anything else her family may need. This mother is so afraid to fail, and as a result of dreading any form of perceived failure, she tends to be obsessive and compulsive with choices in her (and her children's) lives.

Holy Spirit Complex: The keyword is "trust." Individuals with this mother struggle to trust that the Holy Spirit can lead and or guide them. They have learned to be so dependent on self that the idea of trusting the leading of the spirit is terrifying. They may be uncomfortable with expressions of the Holy Spirit and tend to lean toward spiritual environments. They are very structured and controlled. The Holy Spirit is too unpredictable to them and seems to be an unstable part of the faith. They cling to the personhood of Jesus as their safe place in the faith.

The Holy Spirit wants to reveal that God is the ultimate superhero. He wants to debunk the concept of failure and replace it with "lessons learned." There needs to be an acceptance of Proverbs 3: 5-6, which says, *"Trust in the Lord with all your heart and lean not to your understanding. In all your ways, acknowledge Him, and He will direct your paths."*

Wounded Mother: This mother has experienced a lot of pain in her life. She had mottos like "Suck it up and keep going," "You have it better than I did," and "I'm doing the best I can." This mother is giving her children the best she has. Still, she trusts no one and is skeptical about most things. She is guarded and unable to connect with her children interpersonally. She provides their basic needs—food, clothing, and shelter—but she has no idea how to empower and encourage her kids to be the best they can be. That hinders her kids from really getting to know her. She is still struggling to understand herself beyond her pain.

Holy Spirit Complex: The children with this type of mother struggle to believe that the power of the Holy Spirit is living and active inside of them. They fear that they are not enough for the Lord, and that they will mess it all up. They are often gripped with fear and insecurity. These individuals don't adequately express or use their gifts for the Kingdom, because they don't feel like they are enough. 1 John 4:18 says, *"There is no fear in love. But perfect love drives out fear, because fear has to do with punishment. The one who fears is not made perfect in love."* The Holy Spirit is waiting to wrap this individual in love and confidence. The Holy Spirit is waiting to pour out gifts and power on this individual when he or she is ready to receive the Lord's love and acceptance.

Absent/Abusive Mother: The absent/abusive mother is the mother who was not in her child's life physically or emotionally due to addiction, abandonment, denial, and or shame.

Holy Spirit Complex: Children with this type of mother are always questioning and doubting themselves. They are loyal, because they know the pain of not having a mother's comfort and guidance. They love hard and can often place high demands on those in their life. They may live by the "no excuses" motto, which makes others in their life fear letting them down. Forgiveness is critical for the individual dealing with this category of mother. John 14:26 says, *"But the Advocate, the Holy Spirit, whom the Father will send in my name, will teach you all things and will remind you of everything I have said to you."* The Holy Spirit is an advocate and comforter—and comfort is something individuals with absent mothers didn't receive. As a result, they tend to advocate, fight for, and comfort themselves. Matthew 11:28-30 says, *"Come to me, all you who are weary and burdened, and I will give you rest. **29** Take my yoke upon you and learn from me, **for I am gentle and humble in heart, and you will find rest for your souls. 30** For my yoke is easy, and my burden is light."* The key for individuals who have this type of mother to understand is that the Lord desires to deal with the most hurting and delicate parts of us with gentleness. It's His nature, His character. The Holy Spirit longs for you to find rest for your hurting soul. You are not abandoned.

Understanding and releasing how our parents have affected our understanding of God is essential to our ability to establish intimacy with the Lord.

Sin: Sin is another potential roadblock on the journey of intimacy as well as controversial topic in religion. People can become so consumed with the guilt and pain of some of their decisions that it ends up becoming a hindrance to living intimately with the Lord. I want to address it simply:

When you are in a genuine, vulnerable, and transparent relationship with someone, you are committed to honesty to preserve the tie. With that said, an intimate relationship with the Lord allows for revelation, repentance, healing, deliverance, and freedom from anything that can threaten that intimacy. This book is not a dissertation on sin, but rather a proposal, an invitation, and an ideology on an intimate relationship with the Lord. Identifying and repenting from sin has its place in everyone's spiritual journey.

Still, repentance and confession of sin void of intimacy with the Lord are not lasting. These are only temporary religious expressions or emotions.

Intimacy brings forth a contrite heart—a heart willing to turn away from whatever is not beneficial to the individual. Sin, in its essence, separates man from God. But Jesus/Yeshua was sent as an atoning sacrifice for our sin, if we believe Romans 10:9-11, which says, " *If you confess with your mouth, Jesus is Lord, and believe in your heart that God raised him from the dead, you will be saved. For it is with your heart that you believe and are justified, and it is with your mouth that you confess and are saved. Anyone who trusts in Him will never be put to shame."* When we accept Him and engage in a relationship, we are free from the bondage and blockage of sin.

Some of us get stuck in sin; we can't afford for our confessed sin and our secret sins to get in the way of our intimacy. In the previous chapter, I talked about David, and how he was an excellent picture of an intimate relationship with the Lord. I also stated that David was no stranger to sin. Despite his sin, through intimacy with the Lord, he learned how to put sin and guilt in its place. Psalm 103: 10-13: *"10 He does not treat us as our sins deserve or repay us according to our iniquities.11 For as high as the heavens are above the Earth, so great is His love for those who fear Him; 12 As far as the east is from the west, so far has He removed our transgressions from us. 13 As a father has compassion on His children, so the Lord has compassion on those who fear Him."* I couldn't say it better than this. Once we address it, God doesn't hold it over our heads, and neither should we. We have to remember that in the process of repentance and forgiveness, we also have to forgive ourselves. When we do, sin can no longer be a roadblock on our journey to intimacy.

Let me share a practical way to identify which roadblocks you may have to your intimacy with the Lord. Pray this prayer and mean it:

"Lord, I want to hear, see, and sense how you feel about me."

If you begin to hear, see, or feel things that resemble someone or something that hurt you, then you will have a clear indication of precisely what is blocking your intimacy. For example, I did this exercise with someone I was mentoring who was struggling with depression that was consuming her. I asked her to pray that prayer, and when she did, she heard the voice of her mother stating she was not good enough, and she felt the judgment of that in her life. She felt like she did not measure up. At that moment, she realized that those lies were keeping her from intimacy with God. Those lies were the triggers of her depression. She immediately prayed a prayer truly forgiving them—especially the parent who condemned her.

Then, we prayed that same prayer again: *"Lord, I want to see, sense, and hear how you feel about me."* Immediately, she began to cry. For the first time, she felt the warmth and presence of God. It was not something anyone could create; it was a real experience that changed her life and paved the way for intimacy.

God is waiting; sometimes, we just have to get to the place where we acknowledge and accept what's in the way. I am a firm believer in the Sozo ministry. Sozo is the Greek word for "saved, healed, delivered." We all have deep issues we need to work through, and I believe Sozo ministry is one of the most effective ways to free us up for intimacy with God.

CHAPTER 5:

"MY TURNING POINT"

ntimacy with the Lord is an excellent concept for believers. One can understand it, believe in it, and even teach it to others, but *truly being in an intimate relationship with Lord happens when you go from concept to application*. Here is a look at what the process was like for me:

I was pregnant with my daughter Devorah, our "honeymoon baby." She wasn't planned or expected, but she *was* ordained. Before my pregnancy, I was newly married with a complete set of expectations for what a "good wife" should be. I was a program director for a major non-profit organization. I was a young adult pastor at the church I attended. I was speaking to and mentoring young men and women and doing whatever else came my way. Then, all of a sudden, I found out I was pregnant.

Even though Devorah was unexpected, I was still excited to bring her into this world. At the time, I felt like pregnancy didn't need to stop all that I was doing for the Kingdom of God. I was determined to be a ministry superwoman while pregnant, saving the world for Jesus! Well, little did I know, God had other life-altering plans.

During the middle of the first trimester of my pregnancy, I became severely ill. It wasn't the typical morning sickness and early trimester symptoms. My entire body was beginning to shut down, and I couldn't function. The doctors could not figure out what was causing the shut down, and various tests and procedures that needed to be done for diagnosis could not be performed while I was pregnant. So, there I was, unable to DO any of the roles in ministry that validated my faith and maturity as a believer. There I was, unable to fulfill my definition of what a "great wife" looked like. I was sick, shut in, and shut out. The attacks of failure and worthlessness enclosed around me. I knew who the Lord was in his humanity. I knew He wanted an intimate relationship with me, and I had embraced these concepts while I was still doing ministry and seeing results. But now, when no one was watching, while no platform was attainable, I would face the real test of intimacy.

For the first time in my walk with God, I encountered the substance of my relationship with God. What I discovered was terrifying; I was very "successful" in ministry, but just being a daughter of the most high wasn't enough. It was not enough to *say* that it's all about INTIMACY with the Lord. There comes a point in time when we have to ask these questions:

> Are we living content as sons and daughters, or are we trapped in the world's definition of success?
>
> Are we using the word "ministry" to justify our need for man's acceptance and recognition?

This dark place was exactly what I needed, as it also became the turning point of my life. The truth is, I had mastered the rhetoric of intimacy talk, but I was still walking the religious path. This time, it was about getting my attention, getting my mind right, and getting on the road to intimacy. Before this point, I saw the way; I could even talk like I was on the road. But while I frequently visited the outer portions of the road, I wasn't on it. I couldn't feel the dirt from the road—it wasn't between my toes. The wind from the road wasn't in my hair.

So, during that pregnancy, I decided to relinquish all excuses and religious justifications. I was going to fully commit to the journey of intimacy. The Lord began speaking to me, vividly. He gave me the image of a caterpillar in a cocoon. He let me know that He was transforming me into something more beautiful than I could imagine … I just needed to trust Him. And I learned something that has guided my life ever since—that I can only live life one day and one moment at a time. I must be present at this moment to fulfill my task for tomorrow. Matthew 6:25-34 became my mantra:

"25 Therefore I tell you, do not worry about your life, what you will eat or drink; or about your body, what you will wear. Is not life more than food and the body more than clothes? 26 Look at the birds of the air; they do not sow or reap or store away in barns, and yet your heavenly Father feeds them. Are you not much more valuable than they? 27 Can any one of you by worrying add a single hour to your life?

28 And why do you worry about clothes? See how the flowers of the field grow. They do not labor or spin. 29 Yet I tell you that not even Solomon in all his splendor was dressed like one of these. 30 If that is how God clothes the grass of the field, which is here today and tomorrow is thrown into the fire, will he not much more clothe you—you of little faith? 31 So do not worry, saying, 'What shall we eat'? or 'What shall we drink' or 'What shall we wear?' 32 For the pagans run after all these things, and your heavenly Father knows that you need them. 33 But seek first His Kingdom and His righteousness, and all these things will be given to you as well. 34 Therefore do not worry about tomorrow, for tomorrow will worry about itself. Each day has enough trouble of its own."

MY TURNING POINT SAVED MY LIFE!

It became a new season. I decided I wasn't going to take any leadership positions in ministry. I chose not to take any speaking engagements. I knew that, when the time came and the Lord released me from my cocoon, I would be able to soar. I had no idea how long this season was going to be. I was terrified of what I would say when friends and family would call. The truth is, when someone asks us how we are doing, we love to share all of the things we have going on. The things we are doing. Rarely are we transparent enough to just say, "Hey, I'm in a season of just being a daughter or son. I'm taking time to reestablish my intimacy with the Lord, which is more important than what I do." The inability to be free and transparent like this plagues all believers, but it's especially toxic for leaders.

Despite my fear, I took action … and that's what we'll discuss next.

CHAPTER 6:

"MINISTRY FROM THE PLACE OF INTIMACY"

What does it look like when you minister from a place of intimacy? How does real intimacy change the way one does and approaches ministry?

Proverbs 29:25 says, *"Fear of man will prove to be a snare, but whoever trusts in the Lord is kept safe."* I realized that I couldn't do it alone. I needed help. Yet I was afraid of counseling because, in my years of ministry, I believed that the only counsel I required could come from God directly. That is a lie that many Christian leaders believe, and in particular, is a spirit of pride. It comes from a place of feeling severely judged. We struggle to find individuals with whom we can be transparent with and accountable to. And many of us who continuously help others can also manipulate counselors, knowing what to say or do when we know it hasn't been effective. I knew I needed help, but I was skeptical. The Lord knows me better than I know myself, so He knew exactly what and who to set on my path.

I ended up getting a referral to a counselor who did what was called "Theophostic Prayer Counseling." That was the first time I ever heard of it. It is about identifying the source of wounds and evaluating the state of your soul. I reluctantly submitted to the process and learned that Theophostic Prayer Counseling isn't about the counselor. All the counselor is doing is facilitating a place where you receive the truth directly from the Lord; it also has many similarities to SOZO ministry.

During the first day of my counseling, I walked in to find a middle-aged Caucasian pastor as my counselor. Immediately, I sensed there was no way it would work and began putting up walls. As soon as I sat down, the presence of the Lord overwhelmed me. Little did I know my counselor was skilled at handling pastors and leaders in ministry. He was incredibly direct and gentle at the same time; he facilitated an atmosphere that let down all my defenses and allowed me to hear the Lord like never before. I experienced healing in places that I thought were already healed, but had actually only been suppressed. Not only was this counseling necessary for my healing, but I began to realize something so profound … and I want to share it with you.

When leaders lead from places of brokenness, it can have dangerous implications for our ministry. I am in no way saying that we must be perfect to lead. What I *am* saying is that we must be WHOLE to lead. "Whole" means that I have recognized and surrendered the woundedness of my soul, and I have allowed the Lord to come in and uproot all residual effects of my wounds. Being whole means that I am aware of the behaviors and tendencies I have that are a result of pain. I can check, change, and release those tendencies, so they do not influence or get projected onto those I lead. That is ministering from a place of health, not perfection.

On the contrary, many leaders lead and respond to people from their own pain. They justify their actions by over-embellishing the actions of others. The ability to repent quickly and forgive quickly are signs of spiritual maturity, not how many verses you know or how long you have called yourself a "Christian." Intimacy with the Lord is the only place where you experience regular repentance and forgiveness. When we realize how much the Lord puts up with us, it does become more comfortable to extend that same grace toward others.

One of the biggest mistakes we make is the inability to differentiate between having responsibility in ministry and possessiveness. I have found in my experience with ten different churches that it is hard for leaders to share their platforms. Often, the burden we carry as leaders is overwhelming, because we don't empower others to step up. Alternatively, we don't have others who are willing to share the load. When this is the case, there needs to be boundaries in place to keep leaders from being overwhelmed.

Intimacy with the Lord teaches you to know when you need to stand up and work, and it shows you when you need to sit down, so you don't burn out. Intimacy is a filter for the believer; it is a gauge and protection. Religion produces heavy yokes and results in burnout, depression, and harmful habits and addictions to manage stress. As a leader in the church, I felt validated when people complimented me on a message or for putting together a great program or event. I felt a sense of distinguished notoriety when I was mentioned or acknowledged from the pulpit. It gave me worth and a feeling of being needed and accepted. These were all temporary highs that are nice and affirming, but also problematic when leaders look for and need them for validation.

This is not a reprimand of leaders, but rather *a revelation of freedom*! What would it look like, if we were able to do Kingdom work organically, from the place of sons and daughters? What would it look like if we were free from titles and positions … free to flow in love?

Intimacy produces discipleship. Discipleship produces fruit, and fruit nourishes, grows, and sustains the people. When a pastor or leader is absent from the road of intimacy, discipleship suffers or is nonexistent.

When discipleship suffers, the people don't receive the fruit. Instead, they receive freeze-dried, recycled, and processed meals from leaders who don't produce real growth, and the community becomes stagnant. We can't be so busy "religiously" doing God's work that we miss out on doing God's work.

I remember when my husband decided he wanted someone to disciple him. He reached out to the leader of the church we were attending. That leader said he was busy and referred him to another leader under him for my husband to connect with. This particular leader was transitioning from the church, so he was unable to give my husband any discipleship … and therein lies the problem. I will repeat it: we cannot be so busy "religiously" doing God's work that we miss out on doing God's work. If we do not have intimacy, we can't teach intimacy; our best teaching comes from what we emulate.

It is time for the church to produce fruit, so we can become a nourishing source of hope in our communities. Let me give you a few examples of what it looks like practically to lead and do ministry from a place of intimacy.

Motive Check/Narrative:

There are many reasons people choose to take the ministry path. I believe that there are narratives we tell ourselves, which shape our motive for doing ministry. If we are going to minister from a place of intimacy, we must first identify what our narrative is or was, and then examine our motives. If an individual has a narrative that sounds like this—"I have to do ministry because it's what my family has done, and this is who we are,"—the motive is out of fear of obligation. Intimacy says God commands us to love Him and one another and be in a relationship. The Lord doesn't force ministry on His children. Ministry is the use of your gifts for the furthering of the Kingdom of God.

Accountability:

We need to have accountability in our lives. It is essential to understand the difference between "accountability partners" and "friends." Accountability partners are in our lives to speak God's truth to us even when we may not want to hear it. Accountability gives them the right to call you out, speak into decisions, and also sometimes tell you what you should and should not do. An accountability partner must be someone you respect, and someone you know hears from God and is led by the Holy Spirit ... someone who is intimate with the Lord and knows how to go before the Lord on your behalf.

In 2014, I started formally doing life coaching. I was giving people resources and help for years, but at this time in my life, I felt led to venture into it in a formal capacity. My husband and I had the blessing of account-ability partners in our lives, and about a year into life coaching, one of mine was praying for me. She saw a vision of me pregnant with adults; there were all these grown adults connected to me with cords that resembled umbili-cal cords. The fantastic thing is, as soon as she began describing the vision, I knew that the Holy Spirit was speaking through her.

When I started life coaching, I began to carry the healing process of all those I was counseling. I was becoming sick from taking on what the Lord did not intend for me to bear. Even counseling others has to come from a place of intimacy; it's my job to show them the one who can carry their pain; it's not my job to carry the pain. It's easy for leaders in minis-try to move from being the vessel to the source. People can see and feel a leader. Because of this, they tend to place their burdens on leaders as if they are God. When a leader doesn't have intimacy and doesn't have account-ability, they can quickly begin to take a God-like place in others' lives. That is so detrimental to ministry leaders. We need accountability to remind us and keep us in the humble position of being the vessel, not the source.

If you are a leader in ministry, and you have been dealing with unex-plainable sickness or depression, I invite you to ask the Lord, "Am I carrying your children in a way that only you can?" If the Holy Spirit reveals you are, then I want you to pray this prayer:

> *"Father, I repent of getting in the way of you; it wasn't my intent. Somewhere along the way, I became the source and not the vessel. Lord, I choose to release and sever all unhealthy ministry codependency and attachments. Lord, I leave your children before your throne, and I am deciding to prioritize my intimacy with you. I can only lead others to intimacy when I am in the place of intimacy. I love you, and I trust you with your children. They belong to you, not me. Thank you for not giving me more than I can bear, for your yoke is easy and your burden is light.*
>
> *In Yeshua Jesus name, Amen!"*

After praying this prayer, pray that the Lord would send accountability in your life to keep you in the place of being a vessel, not the source.

Results Redefined:

It's human nature to feel that, to deem something worthy or respectful, you need a tangible result. Christian marketing culture says the larger or more popular your ministry is, the more significant the impact for the Kingdom. In this section, I want to redefine what Kingdom results look like through the lens of intimacy.

The best way to measure a result in ministry through the lens of intimacy is found in Galatians 5:22-23: *"But the fruit of the Spirit is love, joy, peace, forbearance, kindness, goodness, faithfulness, 23 gentleness, and self-control. Against such things, there is no law."* The fruit of the Spirit is the manifestation of the character of God in human form. Suppose our ministries are filled with love, joy, Shalom/peace, kindness, and gentleness, and exhibited the ability to show self-control and patience. Then, we can begin to talk about results in a healthy, God-honoring way. Numbers, size, exposure, production, and creativity are not measurable results in the scheme of things. A ministry can have all of those mentioned above and no fruit or character. That would not be Kingdom success, but rather man-approved success. Whether you have unlimited resources or not, the riches are found in the abundance of God's fruit. Where the Lord's fruit is present, his Spirit is also. There is a quote that says, "Don't allow your anointing or talents to take you where your character won't keep you." The author is unknown. Still, I remember hearing that from one of my pastors in California, and it had a lasting impression on me. Intimacy is designed to upend the negative patterns of religion, and how we measure results in ministry must be based on the manifestation of God's character. Everything else flows from that.

CHAPTER 7

"INTIMACY SUSTAINED"

Whenever I receive a life-changing revelation about something, I become so eager to implement every aspect of that revelation, so I can be significant and accomplish greatness. Sometimes, after reading a good book or hearing a good message, whether it is about spirituality, management of weight, or organization in life, I try to become a master of it ... whatever the revelation received.

The intent behind this book is not about mastering "intimacy." It is about recognizing and unlearning negative religious patterns and embracing God's unconditional love for you. The hardest thing to do sometimes is nothing. While learning about the humanity and Jewish culture of Jesus, one of the things I fell in love with was Shabbat.

During Shabbat, the family comes together at a prepared table. There, they light candles and pray to acknowledge that the time together is holy and special. Wine/juice and Challah bread are blessed and taken.

Then the family says specific blessings over one another. Every element of the Shabbat table is an invitation to intimacy.

The Candles: Candles are often used in a romantic context to set the mood and ambiance. They reveal that a particular attitude or countenance is desired. They are relaxing, inviting, and intriguing. The woman of the house prays the Shabbat candle prayer. How interesting that candles are used in Shabbat to kick things off and set the tone the mood for the Sabbath. The Lord wrote the book on romance! I cannot help but feel like He has been showing His children for centuries how He prioritizes intimacy.

The Wine/Challah: This is also communion, but communion during Shabbat is not like any other communion. It is less formal, and more simple and profound. At the table, the mood is set, and God's presence has been ushered in. We take part in the bread that is reflective and symbolic of Yeshua's body that was broken, beaten, and bruised for us. The wine represents His blood that was shed for us and the power that we have in it. During Shabbat, the bread and wine are symbolic of the Lord saying, *"I have given you all of me; every ounce of my being was sacrificed for YOU. I did not withhold any piece of myself from you; that is how much I wanted you to have my love."* The mind-blowing part is that Shabbat was happening during the time Yeshua walked this Earth! People often wonder how Yeshua could do what he did on Calvary. When you understand that Yeshua was in an intimate relationship with God the Father, then you can understand why He was able to bear the cross. He knew confidently that His Father, whom He was intimate with, would not allow Him to experience something if it was not for a higher purpose. He also knew through intimacy that it would pain God the Father to watch His beloved son suffer. Yeshua yearned for what His Father yearned for, which was for all of us to have the opportunity to partake in intimacy with the Father.

The Blessings: If there are issues with anyone in your family and you are at the Shabbat table genuinely, the problems will be rectified before the night is over. During the time of blessings, your guard comes down, and the words of each blessing put things into perspective about marriage and parenting. Consciously taking the time to bless and affirm one another strengthens the family unit and creates an atmosphere of love and support. The blessings are designed to enhance and refuel the passion of the family. In my home, we also like to give affirmations for each other that are specific to the week. For example, I would say to my husband, "Babe, I really appreciate how you affirmed me this week when I was discouraged. Your words were right on time, and I truly felt supported and covered by you." My husband might say to the kids, "The way you all looked out for each other as siblings this week really made me proud as a father." Personalizing the blessings allows for healing to flow within the family.

The Table: A table is a place of intentionality. In American society, various communities use the expression, "I've arrived when I have a seat at the table." That could mean the corporate world executive-level table or some sort of notoriety or popularity. Royal stories and fables often refer to the king's table as a place of royalty and dignity. The table is used metaphorically as a place of acceptance, status, and acknowledgment. It's all so clear when we see it in context. He asks us every week to come and sit with Him at His Shabbat table. He has a place for us—one of acceptance, acknowledgment, and royalty. We are His worthy children … Heirs to his throne through the recognition and acceptance of His sacrifice. There is no more magnificent table than this; there is no table that can compare or compete with this. At the table, there is identity and fulfillment. It is no coincidence that at a table, a couple can decide to spend the rest of their lives together. At a table, kingdoms are united and divided. At a table, every week, an almighty God wants to commune intimately with His children and just be their Father who meets them in their present needs.

Shabbat brings it all together; not one stone is left unturned. Words will not do justice in my attempt to explain how grateful I am to my messianic Jewish brothers and sisters for teaching me how to usher in and observe Shabbat. They gave me a gift that allows me to sustain my intimacy. I am able to come to the Shabbat table and have my flame rekindled with my creator and Lord. It wasn't enough to have a revelation of intimacy. I needed to have this awakening continue, and Shabbat allowed me to realize that there was nothing I could do in my strength to master and perfect intimacy with the Lord. The only way to sustain it was to sit back, relax, and take a seat at HIS table.

In addition to Shabbat there are other Biblical Appointed times that align us with heaven. When we learn from our believing Jewish brothers and sisters and participate in these times, we are deepening our intimacy with the Lord.

Recurring Pain

"Life is a school for the soul. God is the teacher; we are disciples, and suffering is our divinely appointed tutor." This quote from John Parsons, a Messianic scholar, has been an anchor for me during the times in my journey in which I experienced deep pain and trauma. I am now in a place where I deeply love the Lord, and I understand intimacy and purpose. Yet when we are faced with affliction, it has the ability to knock us off of the course of intimacy and place us smack dab in the middle of isolation. Isolation leads to anger, fear, and anxiety, which is a recipe for depression and all other forms of mental illness.

In order to sustain intimacy, we must address how to effectively view recurrences of pain and trauma.

While writing this book, I unexpectedly lost my brother Reggie. He died immediately from a heart attack at work. It was sudden and shocking. I had so many things I wish could have said to him. I wish I could have hugged and kissed him, and said, "See you later." I wish my mother could have held her son's hand. Even as I write these words, the tears come flooding down my face, and I can feel the pain in my stomach.

Grief is a form of traumatic pain that can leave you in a dark place. The key to avoiding this dark place is not found in a deep spiritual revelation, but rather in seven words: invite Yeshua into the place of pain. He never promised us that we wouldn't face difficulty and suffering of various kinds. What He promised was that He would never leave or forsake us in those times.

If you face times when the trauma and pain seem to veer you off the path of intimacy, pray this prayer:

"Abba, I don't have words right now. What I have is sorrow, anger, rage, confusion, and deep pain. Despite these things, I am asking you, pleading before your throne as a son/daughter, to reveal yourself to me in the midst of this pain. Comfort me, and give me the strength to see beyond this place. I trust and know that you will not abandon me in my weakest place. I release all expectations of myself during this time. All I need to be is your son/daughter who can find strength and comfort in the lap of my Father. I release all judgement on how I should or shouldn't process my pain. I choose to trust you in this process, and I will not lean to my own understanding. Forgive me for keeping you from the place you desire to sit with me in the most.

In Yeshua's name, Amen."

Choose Yeshua

If you happen to be reading this and are not a Christian, believer in Jesus/ Yeshua, and/or consider yourself to be an agnostic, spiritual, new age, a universalist, or just a subscriber to whatever feels right, I would like to ask you two questions:

Has your distance or repulsion to Christianity been a result of a family member, friend, leader, teacher, or someone who called themselves

"Christian" hurting or manipulating you? Have you been angered by the hypocrisy of someone who identified themselves as a believer?

If you answered "yes" to either, I want to stop right now and take the time to ask for your forgiveness. I am asking for forgiveness on behalf of anyone who damaged you in the name of Jesus/Yeshua. I ask that you forgive us for failing you and for harming your soul. I also want to ask that you take this moment to give Yeshua a chance.

Take a leap of faith, even if you are unsure.

In my journey, I have tried a little bit of everything, because I didn't like what was on the plate of Christianity. I tried chakras, energy work, crystals, and other gods. I even tried to believe that all I needed was me … that I am my own god and governing force. But placing hope in the universe is just putting faith in a thing that God created.

What I found was that Yeshua was at the center of all those things. Every mantra was a reworded scripture. The Lord is the creator of any positive energy we experience. His Holy Spirit is the conductor of the symphony of energies.

Every way I tried to run, I ended up having a revelation that it was all about the Lord. The most profound one I experienced was that my running from God had nothing to do with Him. I was running from the people and experiences that poorly represented Him.

I know for sure the creator ADONAI, the one who created all things on this Earth, is madly in love with you. He is not looking for PERFECTION, or even the world's standard of success. He wants you for who you are as you are. He never promised us that He would make things in our lives exactly as we want them; He never promised that no one we love would ever die or be hurt. He never promised that we wouldn't experience affliction in this life. What He did promise was to never to leave nor forsake us. HE is ALWAYS there, even when we may not feel it. He is always there, in the deepest, darkest places. I have seen Him work things together for my good, like a master chef in a kitchen. He can handle our questions of "why?" He can handle our anger and rage. He wants to hear from you, and He wants you to hear from Him. If you are willing to accept this dare to be in a relationship not with religion, but with God, then pray this prayer with me:

"Yeshua, son of God, I am uncertain and imperfect. Yet I believe you want to be in a relationship with me, and I am willing to give it a try. I am ready to accept that you love me, you gave your life for me, and that in you, I can do all things. Walk with me. Help me to have the faith to believe that you are who you say you are. Intimacy is new to me, but I am willing to trust you. Reveal yourself to me. I invite you into the depths of my soul. Speak to me, so I can recognize your voice. I believe that your Holy Spirit (Ruach HaKodesh) will lead me and guide me. I choose you, Lord.

In Yeshua's name, Amen."

Welcome to Intimacy.

EPILOGUE

I am currently the President and CEO of a ministry called THE ROAD TO JERUSALEM.

This ministry is about reconciling people to God and each other. Jerusalem is the city of God; getting on the Road to Jerusalem means you are ready to embark on a journey towards the things of God and the ways of God. This journey introduces you to who the Lord is in both his humanity and divinity; this road is about healing, deliverance, and identity in the kingdom; this road also connects you with believing Jews and Gentiles that are all in pursuit of God's kingdom. Intimacy is a project that illuminates what The Road to Jerusalem is all about.

If Intimacy was a blessing for you, I invite you to JOIN THE MOVEMENT.

www.theroadtojerusalem.org

It is my desire to connect you with additional resources that can further your understanding of church history, Jewish believers, and healing. Please feel free to email me at petra@theroadtojerusalem.org for references.

ACKNOWLEDGMENTS

This section recognizes the process of this book and those who contributed to and supported this book specifically.

Intimacy officially started in February 2019; I was on a plane and met a publisher who said he would consult me through self-publishing. I pitched the book to him and let him know that this book has been brewing in me for years; he was moved by the book and began consulting me. By July 2019, I had half of the book written and started a publishing LLC. In late July 2019, my brother Reggie passed away, and this unexpected loss threw our family in a whirlwind. My grief and pain diverted me from the book as I helped my mother and sister-in-law with the arrangements, logistics, and service.

I didn't begin writing again until the end of 2019, and by February of 2020, I completed the first draft of this book, then COVID-19 happened. It affected everything. Any additional projects had to cease, which included Intimacy. I was discouraged but sensed that it wasn't yet time for this book to be released. During the summer of 2020, my husband and I began working for a Church here in Jacksonville for an initiative called the Life Center. The Life Center was like first responder work during the pandemic. We fed anywhere from 500 to 600 families a week all over the city; we had pantries on Monday, Thursday, and Sunday. We were hosting community Shabbat once a month, meeting with families in need and community workers during the week. The book was on pause, and my focus was on Pastoring the hurting during the pandemic. Our initiative shut down in the summer of 2021, and my position shifted. During that shift, I felt led to finish Intimacy and pursue editing. Editing was completed in the late fall of 2021, but I still needed resources for the rest of the self-publishing process.

In November of 2021, something unexpected happened. My father and I began to discuss the transition of leadership for The Road to Jerusalem. We talked about my time frame for becoming President and CEO. We reached a decision, and in December of 2021, the TRTJ board voted for me to be the next President and CEO of the ministry. The transition would be official in April of 2022. In January of 2022, I began a transition process that involved me transitioning from my role at the church and into leading TRTJ full time. While praying about where the Lord wanted me to start with the ministry, He clarified that I needed to complete Intimacy first; He said NOW is the time. It's been a long process, but I am convinced that this is the perfect timing of the Lord for this book to be released.

This book is about relationships. It's about embarking on a journey, and I use my story and experience as a guide. It's an informative memoir of sorts. I hope my transparency inspires others to dig deep and face whatever may be preventing you from pursuing your journey of Intimacy with the Lord.

This book is for anyone and everyone. So, here's to God's perfect timing!

This project would not have been possible without the following people.

Garry, you are my husband, counselor, and best friend. You believed in me from the start and supported me every step of the process. You were super dad to the kids and encouraged me through the ups and downs. You were the first to read the book, and you championed the Lord's work in me in every step. I love you, 240!

Darius, Devorah, and Isaac, thank you for believing in me. Thank you for being patient with mommy. Devorah, thank you for being my honeybee, praying with me, and inspiring me along the way. I pray that this book encourages each of you to pursue your dreams and begin your Intimacy journey with the Lord.

Mom and Dad, from the beginning, you contributed to this project; Dad, the foreword was terrific. You wrote what was in your heart, and I will cherish your words. Mom, thank you for believing that I can do anything! Thank you for your investment and support. I love you both!

Rachel, you never let me quit, you understand my struggles, and you know how to keep me laughing. You write the most amazing words of encouragement I re-read and look to when I need a boost. Thanks for your support and contributions; sis, it's time for Intimacy the album! Kim, My Big sis, we love each other, we get each other, and I love our bond. You have been a blessing in this season of my life in many ways. I appreciate every second of it. Thank you for your contributions and for rooting for me to win. Carmen, My sister-in-love. You are always down for anything Garry and I need. I love you like we share the same blood. You are a light for us when things seem dark, and I am honored to call you sis. Deuce (Matt), Big brother, your talent is beyond description. Thank you for designing the original book cover. It gave me a vision that this was possible! Shira Visser, you believed in me and this book even when I did not and showed support and encouraged me in this project. Thank you for all you gave; I could never thank you enough. Auntie Chanell and Uncle Jermaine, our ride or die Aunt and Uncle. We love the two you and appreciate how you champion us and believe in us. Thank you for your love, support and consistency in our lives.

The first group of contributors for this project were Rachel & Terrance Hughes, Rolanda, and Anthony Locke. Thank you all for supporting the GoFundMe that my husband created. It encouraged me to see others advocating for me.

Judge Earl Clampett, your support came during a time when I was plagued with health issues, and I was deeply discouraged. Your gift was like a smile from heaven saying that everything is going to be ok. Chris Herndon, brother, and friend, you were the anchor in this project. I needed your support to see it through to the finish line, and the Lord used you to do just that. You were a miracle answer to prayer. Thank you, brother, and I pray you are blessed by all this project represents. Larissa Chambers, you are my friend, armor-bearer, and supporter. Your support is like fresh hydration; you understood the assignment of this book, and I wouldn't be here without your help and prayers. I needed you and am so grateful for you. Tai, we've been doing life together since we were 12 and we are still going strong! Thank you for loving me and supporting me in all of life's adventures. You are my sister and I love you! Ransford & Katrina Danquah, fam Garry and I love the Danquah's; we are connected for life. Thank you for believing in us as a unit and sowing into what you see, and thanks for being present. No matter the distance, we have your backs, and we know you have ours! Brother Scotty J, what can I say you are the REAL DEAL Garry and I love and appreciate you more than we can express. You and Misty are family, and we thank you for all that you do. Nathan and Malki our covenant relationship has been a breath of fresh air and we are grateful that the Lord placed us together to do great things for the Kingdom and the best is yet to come! Ed and L'Tonia, when the two of you step in the room things shift!! We are so blessed to call you family and to be seated at the TABLE with you! Tara & Todd, our friendship is sealed in the heavenly book of friendship! Thank you both for your love support and laughter.

Vicki, thank you for connecting me with Megan. I needed an Editor, and she was a God send. Megan, thank you for your professionalism and sensitivity, you are gifted at what you do, and I am so blessed to have you as an editor.

Thank you to all of those who prayed and encouraged me along the way.

Please charge it to my head and not my heart if I missed anyone. There is no way I could have finished this without your Love and Support! From the depths of my heart, Thank You!!!

ABOUT THE AUTHOR

Petra Scott is the President & CEO of The Road to Jerusalem. A ministry of reconciling people to God and each other. Her ministry emphasizes educating believers about Jesus in both his humanity and divinity, which is foundational for an intimate relationship with the Lord. Petra first embraced her call in 2001 when she delivered her first message in South Africa. Since then, she has spoken at conferences, churches, and Messianic synagogues all over the US. She graduated from Azusa Pacific University in 2007 with a degree in Christian Ministry. Petra has over 17 years of experience in ministry. Her passion is to see the entire Body of Believers unified and passionately in love with the Lord. Both Jews and Gentiles.

Petra has experience in both the private and public sectors as a Teacher, Pastor, Consultant, Outreach Director, and Life Coach. Petra is Married to Garry Scott, a fearless man of God and Outreach Pastor; they currently reside in Jacksonville, Florida. They have three exceptional children, Darius, Devorah, and Isaac.